THOUGHTS for YOUNG MEN

Updated Edition with Study Guide

J.C. RYLE

Thoughts for Young Men
Updated Edition) with Study Guide
by J.C. Ryle
© 2013 TheBiblePeople.com

Updated by TheBiblePeople.com

Published by TheBiblePeople.com. Our mission is to encourage people to read, understand, and apply the Bible.

Contents

Introduction

WHEN ST. PAUL wrote his Epistle to Titus about his duty as a minister, he mentioned young men as a class requiring peculiar attention. After speaking of aged men and aged women, and young women, he adds this pithy advice, "Young men likewise exhort to be sober minded" (Tit. 2:6). I am going to follow the Apostle's advice. I propose to offer a few words of friendly exhortation to young men.

I am growing old myself, but there are few things I remember so well as the days of my youth. I have a most distinct recollection of the joys and the sorrows, the hopes and the fears, the temptations and the difficulties, the mistaken judgments and the misplaced affections, the errors and the aspirations, which surround and accompany a young man's life. If I can only say something to keep some young man in the right way, and preserve him from faults and sins, which may mar his prospects both for time and eternity, I shall be very thankful.

There are four things which I propose to do:—

I. I will mention some general reasons why young men need exhorting.

II. I will notice some special dangers against which young men need to be warned.

III. I will give some general counsels which I entreat young men to receive.

IV. I will set down some special rules of conduct which I strongly advise young men to follow.

On each of these four points I have something to say, and I pray God that what I say may do good to some soul.

J.C. Ryle

Church of England bishop, 1880-1900

Chapter 1:
Reasons for Exhorting Young Men

IN THE FIRST place, what are the general reasons why young men need specific exhortation? I will mention several of them in order.

(1) For one thing, there is the painful fact that there are few young men anywhere who seem to be genuine Christians.

I speak without respect of persons; I say it of all. High or low, rich or poor, gentle or simple, learned or unlearned, in town or in country, it makes no matter. I tremble to observe how few young men are led by the Spirit, how few are in that narrow way which leads to life, how few are setting their affections upon things above, how few are taking up the cross, and following Christ. I say it with all sorrow, but I believe, as in God's sight, I am saying nothing more than the truth.

Young men, you form a large and most important class in the population of this country; but where, and in what condition, are your souls? Regardless of where we turn for an answer, the report will be one and the same!

Let us ask any faithful minister of the gospel, and note what he will tell us. How many unmarried young people can he remember who come to the Lord's Supper? Who are the most backward about the doctrines of salvation, the most irregular about Sunday services, the most difficult to draw to weekly Bible studies and prayer meetings, the most inattentive to preaching at all times? Which part of his congregation fills him with most anxiety? Who are the Reubens for whom he has the deepest "searchings of heart"? Who in his flock are the hardest to manage, who require the most frequent warnings and rebukes, who cause him the greatest uneasiness and sorrow, who keep him most constantly in fear for their souls, and seem most hopeless? Depend on it, his answer will always be, "The Young Men."

Let us ask the parents in any county throughout this land, and see what they will generally say. Who in their families give them most pain and trouble? Who need the most watchfulness, and most often exasperate and disappoint them? Who are the first to be led away from what is right, and the last to remember cautions and good advice? Who are the most difficult to keep in order and bounds? Who most frequently break out into open sin, disgrace the name they bear, make their friends unhappy, embitter their older relatives, and cause them to die with sorrow in their hearts? Depend on it, the answer will generally be, "The Young Men."

Let us ask the judges and police officers, and note

what they will reply. Who goes to night clubs and bars most? Who make up mobs and gangs? Who are most often arrested for drunkenness, disturbing the peace, fighting, stealing, assaults, and the like? Who fill the prisons and penitentiaries? Who are the class which requires the most incessant watching and looking after? Depend on it, they will at once point to the same group, they will say, "The Young Men."

Let us turn to the upper classes, and note the report we shall get from them. In one family the sons are always wasting time, health, and money, in the selfish pursuit of pleasure. In another, the sons will follow no profession, and fritter away the most precious years of their life in doing nothing. In another, they take up a profession as a mere form, but pay no attention to its duties. In another, they are always forming wrong connections, gambling, getting into debt, associating with bad companions, keeping their friends in a constant fever of anxiety. Not that rank, and title, and wealth, and education, do not prevent these things! Anxious fathers, and heart-broken mothers, and sorrowing sisters, could tell sad tales about them, if the truth were known. Many a family, with everything this world can give, numbers among its connections some name that is never named, or only named with regret and shame, some son, some brother, some cousin, some nephew, who will have his own way, and is a grief to all who know him.

There is seldom a rich family, which has not got some thorn in its side, some blot in its page of happiness, some constant source of pain and anxiety, and often, far too often, is not this the true cause, "The Young Men"?

What shall we say to these things? These are facts, plain staring facts, facts that meet us on every side, facts which cannot be denied. How dreadful this is! How dreadful the thought, that every time I meet a young man, I meet one who is in all probability an enemy of God, travelling wide road which leads to destruction, unfit for heaven! Surely, with such facts before me, you will not wonder that I exhort you; you must allow there is a good reason.

(2) For another thing, death and judgment is waiting for young men, even as it waits for others, and they nearly all seem to forget it.

Young men, it is appointed for you to die; and however strong and healthy you may be now, the day of your death is perhaps very near. I see young people sick as well as old. I bury youthful corpses as well as aged. I read the names of persons no older than you in every graveyard. I learn from books that, excepting infancy and old age, more die between thirteen and twenty-three than at any other season of life. And yet you live as if you were sure that you will not die at all.

Are you thinking you will pay attention to these things tomorrow? Remember the words of Solomon: "Do not boast about tomorrow, for you do not know what a day may bring" (Prov. 27:1). "I will think about serious things tomorrow," said an unsaved man (Archias, the Theban), to one who warned him of coming danger; but his tomorrow never came. Tomorrow is the devil's day, but today is God's. Satan doesn't care how spiritual your intentions may be, or how holy your resolutions, as long as you determine to act on them tomorrow. Oh, give no place to the devil in this matter! Answer him, "No: Satan! It shall be today—today." All men do not live to be patriarchs, like Isaac and Jacob. Many children die before their fathers. David had to mourn the death of his two finest sons; Job lost all his ten children in one day. Your lot may be like one of theirs, and when death summons, it will be vain to talk of tomorrow, you must go at once.

Are you thinking you will have a more convenient time to think about these things? So thought Felix and the Athenians to whom Paul preached; but it never came. Hell is paved with such ideas. Better make sure to work while you can. Leave nothing unsettled that is eternal. Run no risk when your soul is at stake. Believe me, the salvation of a soul is no easy matter. All need a "great" salvation, whether young or old; all need to be born again, all need to be washed in Christ's blood, all need to be sanctified by the Spirit. Happy is that man who does not leave these things uncertain, but never rests till he has the witness of the Spirit within him, testifying to him that he is a child of God.

Young men, your time is short. Your days are but a brief shadow, a mist that appears for a little while then vanishes, a tale that is soon told. Your bodies are not brass. "Even the young men," says Isaiah, "stumble and fall" (Isa. 40:30). Your health may be taken from you in a moment—it only needs a fall, a fever, an inflammation, a broken blood vessel, and the worm would soon feed upon you in the grave. There is but a step between any one of you and death. This night your soul might be required of you. You are fast going the way of all the earth; you will soon be gone. Your life is all uncertainty, your death and judgment are perfectly sure. You too must hear the Archangel's trumpet, and go forth to stand before the great white throne. You too must obey that summons, which Jerome says was always ringing in his ears: "Get up you dead, and come to judgment." "Surely I am coming soon," is the language of the Judge Himself. I cannot, dare not, will not let you alone.

Oh that you would all take to heart the words of the Preacher: "You who are young, be happy while you are young; and let your heart give you joy in the days of your youth. Follow the ways of your heart and whatever your eyes see, but know that for all these things God will bring you to judgment" (Eccles. 11:9). Amazing, that with such a prospect, any man can be careless and unconcerned! Surely none are so crazy as those who are content to live unprepared to die. Surely the unbelief of men is the most amazing thing in the world. Well may the clearest prophecy in the Bible begin with these words, "Who has believed our message?" (Isa. 53:1). Well may the Lord Jesus say, "When the Son of man comes, will He find faith on the earth?" (Luke 18:8). Young men, I fear lest this be the report of many of you in the courts above: "They will not believe." I fear lest you be hurried out of the world, and awake to find out, too late, that death and judgment are realities. I fear all this, and therefore I exhort you.

(3) For another thing, what young men will be in the future, in all probability depends on what they are now, and they seem to forget this.

Youth is the planting time of adulthood, the molding season in the little space of human life, the turning point in the history of man's mind.

By the shoot that springs ups we can judge the type of tree that is growing, by the blossoms we judge the kind of fruit, by the spring we judge the type of harvest coming, by the morning we judge the coming day, and by the character of the young man, we may generally judge what he will be when he grows up.

Young men, be not deceived. Don't think that you can, at will, serve lusts and pleasures in your beginning, and then go and serve God with ease at your latter end. Don't think you can live with Esau, and then die with Jacob. It is a mockery to deal with God and your souls in such a fashion. It is an awful mockery to suppose you can give the flower of your strength to the world and the devil, and then put off the King of kings with the scraps and leavings of your hearts, the wreck and remnant of your powers. It is an awful mockery, and you may find to your loss that the thing cannot be done.

I daresay you are planning on a late repentance. You don't know what you are doing. You are planning without God. Repentance and faith are the gifts of God, and gifts that He often withholds, when they have been long offered in vain. I grant you true repentance is never too late, but I warn you at the same time, late repentance is seldom true. I grant you, one penitent thief was converted in his last hours, that no man might despair; but I warn you, only one was converted, that no man might presume. I grant you it is written, Jesus is "able also to save completely those that come to God through Him" (Heb. 7:25). But I warn you, it is also written by the same Spirit, "Since you rejected me when I called ... I in turn will laugh at your disaster; I will mock when calamity overtakes you" (Prov. 1:24, 26).

Believe me, you will find it no easy matter to turn to God just when you please. It is a true saying of Archbishop Leighton: "The way of sin is down hill; a man cannot stop when he wants to." Holy desires and serious convictions are not like the servants of the Centurion, ready to come and go at your desire; rather they are like the unicorn in Job, they will not obey your voice, nor attend at your bidding. It was said of the famous general Hannibal of old, when he could have taken the city (Rome) he warred against, he would not, and by and by when he would, he could not. Beware, lest the same kind of event happens to you in the matter of eternal life.

Why do I say all this? I say it because of the force of habit. I say it because experience tells me that people's hearts are seldom changed if they are not changed when young. Seldom indeed are men converted when they are old. Habits have long roots. Once sin is allowed to settle in your heart, it will not be turned out at your bidding. Custom becomes second nature, and its chains are not easily broken. Well says the prophet, "Can the Ethiopian change his skin, or the leopard his spots? Neither can you do good who are accustomed to doing evil" (Jer. 13:23). Habits are like stones rolling down hill, the further they roll, the faster and more ungovernable is their course. Habits, like trees, are strengthened by age. A boy may bend an oak when it is a sapling, but a hundred men cannot root it up when it is a full-grown tree. A child can wade over the Thames River at its source, while the largest ship in the world can float in it when it gets near the sea. So it is with habits: the older, the stronger, the longer they have held possession, the harder they will be to cast out. They grow with our growth, and strengthen with our strength. Custom is the nurse of sin. Every fresh act of sin lessens fear and remorse, hardens our hearts, blunts the edge of our conscience, and increases our evil inclination.

Young men, you may fancy I am laying too much stress on this point. If you had seen old men, as I have done, on the brink of the grave, feelingless, seared, callous, dead, cold, hard as stone, you would not think so. Believe me, you cannot stand still in the affairs of your souls. Habits of good or evil are daily strengthening in your hearts. Every day you are either getting nearer to God, or further off. Every year that you continue unrepentant, the wall of division between you and heaven becomes higher and thicker, and the gulf to be crossed deeper and broader. Oh, dread the hardening effect of constant lingering in sin! Now is the accepted time. See that your decision not be put off until the winter of your days. If you seek not the Lord when young, the strength of habit is such that you will probably never seek Him at all.

I fear this, and therefore I exhort you.

(4) For another thing, the devil uses special diligence to destroy the souls of young men, and they seem not to know it.

Satan knows very well that you will make up the next generation, and therefore he employs every trick to make you his own. I would not have you ignorant of his devices.

You are those on whom he plays off all his choicest temptations. He spreads his net with the most watchful carefulness, to entangle your hearts. He baits his traps with the sweetest morsels, to get you into his power. He displays his wares before your eyes with his utmost ingenuity, in order to make you buy his sugared poisons, and eat his accursed treats. You are the grand object of his attack. May the Lord rebuke him, and deliver you out of his hands.

*Satan knows very well that you
will make up the next generation,
and therefore he employs every
trick to make you his own.*

Young men, beware of being taken by his snares. He will try to throw dust in your eyes, and prevent you seeing anything in its true colors. He would eagerly make you think evil good, and good evil. He will paint, and cover with gold, and dress up sin, in order to make you fall in love with it. He will deform, and misrepresent, and caricature true Christianity, in order to make you take a dislike to it. He will exalt the pleasures of wickedness, but he will hide from you the sting. He will lift up before your eyes the cross and its painfulness, but he will keep out of sight the eternal crown. He will promise you everything, as he did to Christ, if you will only serve him. He will even help you to wear a form of Christianity, if you will only neglect the power. He will tell you at the beginning of your lives, it is too soon to serve God; he will tell you at the end, it is too late. Oh, don't be deceived!

You don't know the danger you are in from this enemy; and it is this very ignorance that makes me afraid. You are like blind men, walking amidst holes and pitfalls; you do not see the perils, which are around you on every side.

Your enemy is mighty. He is called "the Prince of this world" (John 14:30). He opposed our Lord Jesus Christ all through His ministry. He tempted Adam and Eve to eat the forbidden fruit, and so brought sin and death into the world. He tempted even David, the man after God's own heart, and caused his latter days to be full of sorrow. He tempted even Peter, the chosen Apostle, and made him deny his Lord. Surely his hostility towards God and man is to be despised.

Your enemy is restless. He never sleeps. He is always going about as a roaring lion, seeking whom he may devour. He is continually going to and fro in the earth, and walking up and down in it. You may be careless about your souls: he is not. He wants them to make them miserable, like himself, and will have them if he can. Surely his hatred towards God and man is to be despised.

And your enemy is cunning. For nearly six thousand years he has been reading one book, and that book is the heart of man. He ought to know it well, and he does know it—all its weakness, all its deceitfulness, all its folly. And he has a store of temptations, those that are most likely to do the heart harm. Never will you go to the place where he will not find you. Go into towns, he will be there. Go into a wilderness, he will be there also. Sit among drunkards and partiers, and he will be there to help you. Listen to preaching, and he will be there to distract you. Surely such ill will is to be despised.

Young men, this enemy is working hard for your destruction, however little you may think it. You are the prize for which he is specially contending. He foresees you must either be the blessings or the curses of your day, and he is trying hard to lodge himself in your hearts early, in order that you may help forward his kingdom by and by. Well does he understand that to spoil the bud is the surest way to ruin the flower.

Oh that your eyes were opened, like those of Elisha's

servant in Dothan! Oh that you would see how Satan is scheming against your peace! I must warn you, I must exhort you. Whether you will hear or not, I cannot, dare not, leave you alone.

(5) For another thing, young men need exhorting, because of the sorrow it will save them, to begin serving God now.

Sin is the mother of all sorrow, and no sort of sin appears to give a man so much misery and pain as the sins of his youth. The foolish acts he did, the time he wasted, the mistakes he made, the bad company he kept, the harm he did himself—both body and soul—the chances of happiness he threw away, the openings of usefulness he neglected, all these are things that often embitter the conscience of an old man, throw a gloom on the evening of his days, and fill the later hours of his life with self-reproach and shame.

Some men could tell you of the untimely loss of health, brought on by youthful sins. Disease racks their limbs with pain, and life is almost a weariness. Their muscular strength is so wasted, that the slightest weight seems a burden. Their eye has become prematurely dim, and their natural energy abated. The sun of their health has gone down while it is yet day, and they mourn to see their flesh and body consumed. Believe me, this is a bitter cup to drink.

Others could give you sad accounts of the consequences of idleness. They threw away the golden opportunity for learning. They would not get wisdom at the time when their minds were most able to receive it, and their memories most ready to retain it. And now it is too late. They have no time to sit down and learn. They no longer have the same power, even if they had the time. Lost time can never be redeemed. This too is a bitter cup to drink.

Others could tell you of grievous mistakes in judgment, from which they suffer all their lives long. They would have their own way. They would not take advice. They formed some connection that has been altogether ruinous to their happiness. They chose a profession for which they were entirely unsuited. And they see it all now. But their eyes are only open when the mistake cannot be retrieved. Oh, this is also a bitter cup to drink!

Young men, young men, I wish you could know the comfort of a conscience not burdened with a long list of youthful sins. These are the wounds that pierce the deepest. These are the arrows that drink up a man's spirit. This is the iron that enters into the soul. Be merciful to yourselves. Seek the Lord early, and so you will be spared many a bitter tear.

This is the truth that Job seems to have felt. He says, "You write down bitter things against me, and make me inherit the sins of my youth" (Job 13:26). So also his friend Zophar, speaking of the wicked, says, "His bones are full of the sin of his youth, which shall lie down with him in the dust" (Job 20:11).

David also seems to have felt it. He says to the

Lord, "Remember not the sins of my youth, nor my transgressions" (Ps. 25:7).

Go and ask believers now, and I think many of them will tell you much the same. "Oh that I could live my young days over again!" he will most probably say. "Oh that I had spent the beginning of my life in a better fashion! Oh that I had not laid the foundation of evil habits so strongly in the spring-time of my journey!"

Young men, I want to save you all this sorrow, if I can. Hell itself is truth known too late. Be wise in time. What youth sows, old age must reap. Don't give the most precious season of your life to that which will not comfort you in the latter days of your life. Instead, sow for yourselves that which will result in righteousness. Break up your hard ground, and don't sow among thorns.

Sin may come easily to your hands, or run smoothly off your tongue now, but depend on it: sin and you will meet again by and by, however little you may like it. Old wounds will often ache and give pain long after they are healed and only a scar remains—so may you find it with your sins. The footprints of animals have been found on the surface of rocks that were once wet sand, thousands of years after the animal that made them has perished and passed away—so also it may be with your sins.

"Experience," says the proverb, "is a hard school to attend, but fools will learn in no other." I want you all to escape the misery of learning in that school. I want you to avoid the wretchedness that youthful sins are sure to entail. This is the last reason why I exhort you.

Study Guide on Chapter 1

1. The author gives five reasons for exhorting young men. What are they? (List them.)

2. How would your parents describe you and your spiritual life?

3. How would the people at school describe you and your spiritual life?

4. Ryle says that if you asked pastors, parents in churches, law enforcement, and the wealthy in general, that they would say that those most inclined to turn from God and his ways and to revel in sin are "The Young Men." To what extent do you agree or disagree with this?

5. Ryle makes the statement: "Tomorrow is the devil's day, but today is God's." What does he mean by this?

6. What kinds of things do you tend to put off until "tomorrow"? Give three examples.

7. What does Ryle have to say about the "force of habit" in relation to sin?

8. What sin have you allowed to take root in your heart?

9. Ryle talks about how the devil makes a special effort to destroy the souls of young men, yet they are largely unaware of this. Give an example of a godly person from the Bible who Satan successfully tempted.

10. Ryle speaks about the sorrow that men feel in their later years as a consequence of the actions of their youth. In this, he speaks not only of the "bad things" they did in their youth, but also about the "good things" they failed to do. How do you think both of these types of actions would burden a person's conscience?

11. Near the end of the chapter, the author uses a metaphor to make a point: "What youth sows, old age must reap. Don't give the most precious season of your life to that which will not comfort you in the latter days of your life. Sow to yourselves rather in righteousness: break up your hard ground, don't sow among thorns." What does he mean by this?

Chapter 2:
Dangers of Young Men

IN THE SECOND place, there are some special dangers against which young men need to be warned.

(1) One danger to young men is pride.

I know well that all souls are in fearful peril. Old or young, it matters not: all have a race to run, a battle to fight, a heart to humble, a world to overcome, a body to keep under control, a devil to resist. And we may well say, *Who is sufficient for these things?* But still every age and condition has its own peculiar snares and temptations, and it is well to know them. He that is forewarned is forearmed. If I can only persuade you to be on your guard against the dangers I am going to name, I am sure I shall do your souls an essential service.

Pride is the oldest sin in the world. Indeed, it was before the world. Satan and his angels fell by pride. They were not satisfied with their first situation and status. Thus pride stocked hell with its first inhabitants.

Pride cast Adam out of paradise. He was not content with the place God assigned him. He tried to raise himself, and fell. Thus sin, sorrow, and death entered in by pride.

Pride sits in all our hearts by nature. We are born proud. Pride makes us rest satisfied with ourselves, think we are good enough as we are, keep us from taking advice, refuse the gospel of Christ, turn every one to his own way. But pride never reigns anywhere so powerfully as in the heart of a young man.

How common is it to see young men with big heads, high-minded, and not wanting to hear wise counsel! How often they are rude and uncourteous to all around them, thinking they are not valued and honored as they deserve! How often they will not stop to listen to a hint from an older person! They think they know everything. They are full of conceit of their own wisdom. They view elderly people, especially their relations, as stupid, and dull, and slow. They don't think they are in need of teaching or instruction for themselves; they think they understand all things. It makes them almost angry to be spoken to. Like young horses, they cannot bear the least control. They must be independent, and have their own way. They seem to think, like those whom Job mentioned, "[We] are the people, and wisdom shall die with us" (Job 12:2). And this is all pride.

Such a one was Rehoboam, who despised the counsel of the old experienced men who stood before his father, and listened to the advice of the young men of his own generation. He lived to reap the consequences of his folly. There are many like him.

Such a one was the prodigal son in the parable, who

27

wanted to have his share of the inheritance, and set up for himself the kind of life he desired. He could not submit to live quietly under his father's roof, but would go into a far country, and be his own master. Like the little child that will leave its mother's hand and walk alone, he soon felt the sting of his folly. He became wiser when he had to eat husks with the pigs. But there are many like him.

Young men, I beseech you earnestly, beware of pride. Two things are said to be very rare sights in the world: one is a young man humble, and the other is an old man content. I fear this saying is only too true.

Don't be proud of your own abilities, your own strength, your own knowledge, your own appearance, or your own cleverness. Don't be proud of yourself, and your endowments of any kind. It all comes from not knowing yourself and the world. The older you grow, and the more you see, the less reason you will find for being proud. Ignorance and inexperience are the pedestal of pride; once the pedestal is removed, pride will soon come down.

Remember how often Scripture sets before us the excellence of a humble spirit. How strongly we are warned "not to think of [ourselves] more highly than [we] ought to think"! (Rom. 12:3). How plainly we are told, "The man who thinks he knows something does not yet know as he ought to know"! (1 Cor. 8:2). How strict is the command, "Clothe yourselves with humility"! (Col. 3:12). And again, "Be clothed with humility" (1 Pet. 5:5). Alas, this is a garment of which many seem not to have so much as a rag.

Think of the great example our Lord Jesus Christ leaves us in this respect. He washed the feet of His disciples, saying, "You should do as I have done for you" (John 13:15). It is written, "Though He was rich, yet for your sakes He became poor" (2 Cor. 8:9). And again, "[He] made Himself nothing, taking the very nature of a servant, being made in human likeness. And being found in appearance as a man, He humbled Himself" (Phil. 2:7, 8). Surely to be proud is to be more like the devil and fallen Adam, than like Christ.

Think of the wisest man that ever lived—I mean Solomon. See how he speaks of himself as a "little child,"—as one who "[knew] not how to go out or come in," or manage for himself (1 Kings 3:7). That was a very different spirit from his brother Absalom's, who thought himself equal to anything: "Oh that I were made judge in the land! Then everyone who has a complaint or case would come to me and see that he gets justice." (2 Sam. 15:4). That was a very different spirit from his brother Adonijah's, who "exalted himself, saying, 'I will be king' " (1 Kings 1:5). Humility was the beginning of Solomon's wisdom. He writes it down as his own experience, "Do you see a man who is wise in his own eyes? There is more hope for a fool than for him" (Prov. 26:12).

Young men, take to heart the Scriptures quoted here. Do not be too confident in your own judgment. Stop being so sure that you are always right, and others wrong. Distrust your own opinion, when you find it contrary to that of older men than yourselves, and especially to that of your own parents. Age gives experience, and therefore deserves respect. It is a mark of Elihu's wisdom, in the book of Job, that he "waited till Job had spoken, because they were older than he" (Job 32:4). And afterwards he said, "I am young, and you are very old; therefore I was afraid, and did not dare to tell you what I know. I thought, 'Age should speak, and those of advanced years should teach wisdom' " (Job 32:6,7). Modesty and silence are beautiful graces in young people. Never be ashamed of being a learner. Jesus was one at twelve years of age when He was found in the temple "sitting in the midst of the teachers, both hearing them, and asking them questions" (Luke 2:46). The wisest men would tell you they are always learners, and are humbled to find after all how little they know. The great Sir Isaac Newton used to say that he felt himself no better than a little child, who had picked up a few precious stones on the shore of the sea of knowledge.

Young men, if you would be wise, if you would be happy, remember the warning I give you: Beware of pride.

(2) Another danger to young men is the love of pleasure.

Youth is the time when our passions are strongest and, like unruly children, cry most loudly for indulgence. Youth is the time when we generally have most health and strength. Death seems far away, and to enjoy ourselves in this life seems everything. Youth is the time when most people have few earthly cares or anxieties to take up their attention. And all these things help to make young men think of nothing so much as pleasure. "I serve lusts and pleasures." That is the true answer many a young man should give, if asked, "Whose servant are you?"

Young men, time would fail me if I were to tell you all the fruits this love of pleasure produces, and all the ways in which it may do you harm. Why should I speak of partying, feasting, drinking, gambling, theatre going, dancing, and the like? Few are to be found who do not know something of these things by bitter experience. And these are only instances. All things that give a feeling of excitement for the time, all things that drown thought, and keep the mind in a constant whirl, all things that please the senses and gratify the flesh, these are the sort of things that have mighty power at your time of life, and they owe their power to the love of pleasure. Be on your guard. Don't be like those of whom Paul speaks: "Lovers of pleasure more than lovers of God" (2 Tim. 3:4).

Remember what I say: if you cling to earthly pleasures, these are the things that murder souls. There is no surer way to get a seared conscience and a hard heart, than to give way to the desires of the flesh and mind. It seems like nothing at first, but it takes its toll in the long run.

There is no surer way to get a seared conscience and a hard heart, than to give way to the desires of the flesh and mind. It seems like nothing at first, but it takes its toll in the long run.

Consider what Peter says: "Abstain from fleshly lusts, which war against the soul" (1 Pet. 2:11). They destroy the soul's peace, break down its strength, lead it into hard captivity, and make it a slave.

Consider what Paul says: "Put to death whatever belongs to your earthly nature: sexual immorality, impurity, lust, evil desires, and greed" (Col. 3:5). "Those that belong to Christ have crucified the sinful nature with its passions and desires" (Gal. 5:24). Once the body was a perfect mansion of the soul, now it is all corrupt and disordered, and needs constant watching. It is a burden to the soul, not a helper—a hindrance, not an assistance. It may become a useful servant, but it is always a bad master.

Consider, again, the words of Paul: "Clothe yourselves with the Lord Jesus Christ, and do not think about how to gratify the sinful nature" (Rom. 13:14). "These," says Leighton, "are the words, the very reading of which gave Augustine such a great conviction of heart, causing an immoral young man to be turned into a faithful servant of Jesus Christ." Young men, I wish this might be the case with all of you.

Remember, again, if you cling to earthly pleasures, they are all unsatisfying, empty, and meaningless. Like the locusts of the vision in Revelation, they seem to have crowns on their heads; but like the same locusts, you will find they have stings, real stings, in their tails. All is not gold that glitters. All is not good that tastes sweet. All is not real pleasure that pleases for a time.

Go and take your fill of earthly pleasures if you will—you will never find your heart satisfied with them. There will always be a voice within, crying, like the leech in the Proverbs, "Give, give!" There is an empty place there, which nothing but God can fill. You will find, as Solomon did by experience, that earthly pleasures are but a meaningless show—promising contentment but bringing a dissatisfaction of spirit—like gold-plated caskets that are beautiful on the outside but full of ashes and corruption within. Better to be wise in your youth. Better to write the word "poison" on all earthly pleasures. The most lawful of them must be used with moderation. All of them are soul-destroying if you give them your heart.

And here I will not shrink from warning all young men to remember the seventh commandment: to beware of adultery and sexual immorality, of all impurity of every kind. I fear that we don't speak plainly often enough on this part of God's law. But when I see how prophets and Apostles have dealt with this subject, when I see the number of young men who walk in the footsteps of Reuben, and Hophni, and Phinehas, and Amnon, I for one cannot, with a good conscience, hold my peace. The world becomes more wicked because of our failure to teach and preach on this commandment. For my own part, I feel it would be false and unscriptural delicacy, in addressing young men, not to speak of that which is pre-eminently "the young man's sin."

The violation of the seventh commandment is the sin above all others, that, as Hosea says, "takes away understanding" (Hos. 4:11). It is the sin that leaves deeper scars upon the soul than any sin that a man can commit. It is a sin that slays its thousands in every age, and has overthrown more than a few of the saints of God in the past. Lot, and Samson, and David are fearful examples. It is the sin that man dares to smile at, and smooths over using the terms: thrills, love, uncontrollable passions, and natural desires. But it is the sin that the devil particularly rejoices over, for he is the "unclean spirit;" and it is the sin that God abhors, and declares He "will judge" (Heb. 13:4).

Young men, "flee from sexual immorality" (1 Cor. 6:18) if you love life. "Let no man deceive you with empty words, for because of such things God's wrath comes on those who are disobedient" (Eph. 5:6). Flee from the opportunity of it—from the company of those who might draw you into it—from the places where you might be tempted to it. Be like holy Job: Make a covenant with your eyes not to look lustfully at a woman (Job 31:1). Flee from talking of it. It is one of the things that shouldn't even be hinted at in conversation. You cannot touch black grease without getting your hands dirty. Flee the thoughts of it; resist them, destroy them, pray against them—make any sacrifice rather than give way to them. Imagination is the hotbed where this sin is too often hatched. Guard your thoughts, and there will be little to fear about your actions.

Consider the caution I have been giving. If you forget all else, do not let this be forgotten.

(3) Another danger to young men is thoughtlessness and inconsideration.

Lack of thought is one simple reason why thousands of souls are cast away forever. Men will not consider, will not look ahead, will not look around them, will not reflect on the end of their present course, and the sure consequences of their present ways, and awake at last to find they are damned for lack of thinking.

Young men, none are in more danger of this than yourselves. You know little of the perils around you, and so you are careless how you walk. You hate the trouble of sober, quiet thinking, and so you make wrong decisions and bring upon yourselves much sorrow. Young Esau had to have his brother's stew and sold his birthright to get it; he never thought how much he would one day want it. Young Simeon and Levi wanted to avenge their sister Dinah by slaying the Shechemites; they never considered how much trouble and anxiety they might bring on their father Jacob and his house by doing so. Job seems to have been especially afraid of this thoughtlessness among his children. It is written, that when they had a feast, and "the days of their feasting had runt their course, Job sent and had them purified. He rose up early in the morning and offered a burnt offering for each of them, thinking, 'It may be that my sons have sinned, and cursed God in their hearts.' This was Job's regular custom" (Job 1:5).

Believe me, this world is not a world in which we can do well without thinking, and least of all do well in the matter of our souls. "Don't think," whispers Satan; he knows that an unconverted heart is like a dishonest businessman's financial records—it will not bear close inspection. "Consider your ways," says the Word of God. Stop and think; consider and be wise. Well says the Spanish proverb, "Hurry comes from the devil." Just as men marry in a rush and then are miserable for the rest of their lives, so they make mistakes about their souls in a minute, and then suffer for it for years. Just as a bad servant does wrong, and then says, "I never gave it a thought," so young men run into sin, and then say, "I did not think about it; it did not look like sin." Not look like sin! What would you expect? Sin will not come to you, saying, "I am sin;" it would do little harm if it did. Sin always seems "good, and pleasant, and desirable," at the time of commission. Oh, get wisdom! Get discretion! Remember the words of Solomon: "Give careful thought to the paths of your feet, and be steadfast in all your ways" (Prov. 4:26).

Some, I dare say, will object—saying that what I am asking is unreasonable, that youth is not the time of life when people ought to be grave and thoughtful. I answer that there is little danger of their being too much so in the present day. Foolish talking, and kidding, and joking, and excessive merriment are only too common. I don't argue the fact that there is a time for all things, but to be always joking and flippant is anything but wise. What says the wisest of men? "It is better to go to the house of mourning, than to go to the house of feasting: for death is the destiny of all men; and the living should take this to heart. Sorrow is better than laughter: because a sad face is good for the heart. The heart of the wise is in the house of mourning; but the heart of fools is in the house of pleasure" (Eccles. 7:2-4). Matthew Henry tells a story of a great statesman in Queen Elizabeth's time, who retired from public life in his latter days, and gave himself up to serious thought. His former merry companions came to visit him, and told him he was becoming melancholy. "No," he replied, "I am serious; for all are serious round about me. God is serious in observing us, Christ is serious in interceding for us, the Spirit is serious in striving with us, the truths of God are serious, our spiritual enemies are serious in their endeavors to ruin us, poor lost sinners are serious in hell, and why then should not you and I be serious too?"

Oh, young men, learn to be thoughtful! Learn to consider what you are doing, and where you are going. Make time for calm reflection. Commune with your own heart, and be still. Remember my caution: Do not be lost merely because of a lack of thought.

(4) Another danger to young men is contempt of true Christianity.

This also is one of your special dangers. I always observe that none pay so little outward respect to Christianity as young men. None take so little part in church services—when they are present at them—use their Bibles so little, sing so little, listen to preaching so little. None are so generally absent at prayer meetings, and Bible studies, and all other weekday helps to the soul. Young men seem to think they do not need these things; they may be good for women and old men, but not for them. They appear ashamed of seeming to care about their souls. One would almost fancy they reckoned it a disgrace to go to heaven at all. And this is contempt of Christianity. It is the same spirit that made the young people of Bethel mock Elisha, and of this spirit I say to all young men: Beware! If it is worthwhile to be a Christian, then it is worthwhile to be in earnest about it.

Contempt of holy things is the straight road to hell. Once a man begins to make a jest and joke of any part of Christianity, then I am never surprised to hear that he has turned out to really be an unbeliever in his heart.

Young men, have you really made up your minds about this? Have you clearly looked into the dangers that lie before you, if you persist in despising Christianity? Call to mind the words of David: "The fool says in his heart, 'There is no God' " (Ps. 14:1). The fool, and no one but the fool has said it, but he has never proved it! Remember, if ever there was a book that has been proved true from beginning to end, by every kind of evidence, that book is the Bible. It has defied the attacks of all enemies and faultfinders. The Word of the LORD is indeed proven true (Ps. 18:30). It has been tested in every way, and the more it has been tested, the more evidently has it been shown to be the very handiwork of God Himself. What will you believe, if you do not believe the Bible? There is no choice but to believe something ridiculous and absurd. Depend on it, no man is so grossly naive as the man who denies the Bible to be the Word of God; and if it be the Word of God, be careful that you don't despise it.

Men may tell you there are difficulties in the Bible, things hard to understand. It would not be God's book if there were not. And what if there are? You don't despise medicines because you cannot explain all that your doctor does with them. But whatever men may say, the things needed for salvation are as clear as daylight. Be very sure of this, people never reject the Bible because they cannot understand it. They understand it only too well. They understand that it condemns their own behavior; they understand that it witnesses against their own sins, and summons them to judgment. They try to believe it is false and useless, because they don't want to admit that it is true. "Men question the truth of Christianity," says South, "because they hate the practice of it."

Young men, when did God ever fail to keep His word? Never. What He has said, He has always done; and what He has spoken, He has always made good. Did He fail to keep His word at the flood? No. Did He fail with Sodom and Gomorrah? No. Did He fail with unbelieving Jerusalem?

If it is worthwhile to be a Christian, then it is worthwhile to be in earnest about it.

No. Has He failed with the Jews up to this very hour? No. He has never failed to fulfil His word. Take care, lest you be found among those who despise God's Word.

Never laugh at Christianity. Never make a joke of sacred things. Never mock those who are serious and earnest about their souls. The time may come when you will count those happy whom you laughed at—at a time when your laughter will be turned into sorrow, and your mockery into seriousness.

(5) Another danger to young men is the fear of man's opinion.

"The fear of man will prove to be a snare" (Prov. 29:25). It is terrible to observe the power that it has over most minds, and especially over the minds of the young. Few seem to have any opinions of their own, or to think for themselves. Like dead fish, they go with the stream and tide. What others think is right, they think is right. What others call wrong, they call wrong too. There are not many original thinkers in the world. Most men are like sheep; they follow a leader. If it was the fashion of the day to be Roman Catholics, they would be Roman Catholics; if it was the fashion to be Islamic, they would be Islamic. They dread the idea of going against the current of the times. In a word, the opinion of the day becomes their religion, their creed, their Bible, and their God.

The thought, "What will my friends say or think of me?" nips many a good inclination in the bud. The fear of being looked at, laughed at, or ridiculed, prevents many a good habit from being taken up. There are Bibles that would be read this very day, if the owners dared. They know they ought to read them, but they are afraid: "What will people say?" There are knees that would be bent in prayer this very night, but the fear of man forbids it: "What would my wife, my brother, my friend, my companion say, if they saw me praying?" Oh, what wretched slavery this is, and yet how common! "I feared the people," said Saul to Samuel, and so he broke the commandment of the Lord (1 Sam. 15:24). "I am afraid of the Jews," said Zedekiah, the graceless king of Judah, and so he disobeyed the advice which Jeremiah gave him (Jer. 38:19). Herod was afraid of what his guests would think of him, so he did that which made him "exceedingly sorry"—he beheaded John the Baptist. Pilate feared offending the Jews, so he did that which he knew in his conscience was unjust—he delivered up Jesus to be crucified. If this isn't slavery, what is?

Young men, I want you all to be free from this bondage. I want you each to care nothing for man's opinion, when the path of duty is clear. Believe me, it is a great thing to be able to say "No!" Here was good King Jehoshaphat's weak point: he was too easy and yielding in his dealings with Ahab, and therefore caused many of his troubles (1 Kings 22:4). Learn to say "No!" Do not let the fear of not seeming good-natured make you unable to do it. When sinners entice you, be able to say decidedly, "I will not give in to them" (Prov. 1:10).

Consider how unreasonable this fear of man is. How short-lived is man's hostility, and how little harm he can do you! "Who are you, that you should be afraid of a man that will die, and of the son of man, which is like the grass: and forget the LORD your Maker, who has stretched forth the heavens, and laid the foundations of the earth?"(Isaiah 51:12, 13). And how thankless is this fear! None will really think better of you for it. The world always respects those most who act boldly for God. Oh, break these bonds, and cast these chains from you! Never be ashamed of letting men see you want to go to heaven. Do not think it a disgrace to show that you a servant of God. Never be afraid of doing what is right.

Remember the words of the Lord Jesus: "Do not be afraid of those who kill the body but cannot kill the soul. Rather be afraid of the One who can destroy both soul and body in hell" (Matt. 10:28). Try only to please God, and He can soon make others pleased with you. "When a man's ways please the LORD, he makes even his enemies live at peace with him" (Prov. 16:7).

Young men, be of good courage. Don't worry what the world says or thinks; you will not always be with the world. Can man save your soul? No. Will man be your judge in the great and dreadful day of judgment? No. Can man give you a good conscience in life, a good hope in death, a good answer in the morning of resurrection? No! No! No! Man can do nothing of the sort. Then "fear not the reproach of men, neither be afraid of their insults: for the moth shall eat them up like a garment, and the worm shall eat them like wool" (Isa. 51:7,8). Call to mind the saying of Gardiner: "I fear God, and therefore I have none else to fear." Go and be like him.

Such are the warnings I give you. Take them to heart. They are worth thinking over. I am much mistaken if they are not greatly needed. The Lord grant that they may not have been given to you in vain.

Young men, be of good courage.
Don't worry what the world says
or thinks; you will not always be
with the world.

Study Guide on
Chapter 2

1. Ryle writes: "Every age and condition has its own peculiar snares and temptations, and it is well to know them. He that is forewarned is forearmed". In light of this, he addresses five dangers against which young men particularly need to be warned. List them.

2. In the beginning of chapter 2, Ryle gives a variety of definitions and descriptions of how pride shows itself in young men. In what ways do you see these in the young men around you at school, in your neighborhood, on your sports teams and at church?

3. Ryle points out the Bible's command to "clothe yourself with humility" (Col. 3:12, I Peter 5:5). Name three things that would be different about you if you followed this command this next week.

4. Ryle urges you to "never be ashamed of being a learner." Why is it hard to admit that you don't know everything – that you aren't always right?

5. What do you think Mr. Ryle means when he says "love of pleasure"? (This is related to what the

apostle Paul meant in 2 Timothy 3:4 when he spoke of men who were "lovers of pleasure.")

6. Are there things that you do just for the thrill? Do you play games or participate in activities to "get a rush"? List two things you do just for a thrill?

7. At face value, thrill seeking is not wrong. However, in relation to earthly pleasures, Ryle says, "the most lawful of them must be used with moderation. All of them are soul-destroying if you give them your heart." Why would he say that something that feels good and enjoyable could damage your soul?

8. Ryle gives a specific warning in relation to the Seventh Commandment: He urges young men to beware of adultery, sexual immorality, and of all impurity of every kind. This warning includes a wide variety of sexually related issues and sins, not just the act of sex outside of marriage. What other issues and sins do you think this warning might address?

9. At the end of chapter 2 – section 2, Ryle challenges young men with Paul's command to "flee sexual immorality," and he gives three specifics related to fleeing: First, flee the opportunity for it. Second, flee from talking about it. Third, Flee from thoughts related to it. How can you specifically put these three aspects of "fleeing" into practice in your own life? Give one example for each.

10. At the beginning of chapter 2 – section 3, Ryle writes: " 'Don't think,' whispers Satan." Why would Satan want you not to think?

11. Ryle advises: "Young men, learn to be thoughtful! Learn to consider what you are doing and where you are going. Make time for calm reflection. Commune with your own heart, and be still. Remember my caution—do not be lost merely for the lack of thought." How would your life be different if you followed this advice?

12. What do you think of this quote: "If it is worthwhile to be a Christian, then it is worthwhile to be in earnest about it."

13. Ryle quotes Proverbs 29:25, which says, "The fear of man will prove to be a snare," and he makes the point that the fear of man will enslave you. He says that the thought *"What will my friends say or think of me?"* leads to bondage. How have you seen this truth put on display in the lives of other young men (at school, in your neighborhood, at church, at camp...)?

14. How have you seen this in your own life?

15. At the end of chapter 2, Ryle offers encouraging words for how to be free of this kind of bondage. What did you find most encouraging or challenging?

Do not let the devil succeed in persuading you that sin is a small matter!

Chapter 3:
General Counsels to Young Men

IN THE THIRD place, I wish to give some general counsels to young men.

(1) For one thing, try to get a clear view of the evil of sin.

Young men, if you only knew what sin is, and what sin has done, you would not think it strange that I exhort you as I do. You do not see it in its true colors. Your eyes are naturally blind to its guilt and danger, and so you cannot understand what makes me so worried about you. Do not let the devil succeed in persuading you that sin is a small matter!

Think for a moment what the Bible says about sin: how it dwells naturally in the heart of every man and woman alive (Eccles. 7:20; Rom. 3:23), how it continually defiles our thoughts, words, and actions (Gen. 6:5; Matt. 15:19), how it renders us all guilty and abominable in the sight of a holy God (Isa. 64:6; Hab. 1:13), how it leaves us utterly without hope of salvation, if we look to ourselves (Ps. 143:2; Rom. 3:20), how its fruit in this world is shame, and its wages in the world to come is death (Rom. 6:21, 23). Think calmly about all this. I tell you this: It is just as sad to be dying of cancer and not to know it, as it is to be a living man, and not know it.

Think what an awful change sin has worked on all our natures. Man is no longer what he was when God formed him out of the dust of the ground. He came out of God's hand upright and sinless (Eccles. 7:29). In the day of his creation he was, like everything else, "very good" (Gen. 1:31). And what is man now? A fallen creature, a ruin, a being that shows the marks of corruption all over, his heart like Nebuchadnezzar, degraded and earthly, looking down and not up, his affections like a household in disorder, calling no man master, all extravagance and confusion, his understanding like a lamp flickering in the socket, powerless to guide him, not knowing good from evil, his will like a rudderless ship, tossed to and fro by every desire, and constant only in choosing any way rather than God's. What a wreck man is compared to what he might have been! We may understand such figures being used as blindness, deafness, disease, sleep, death, when the Spirit has to give us a picture of man as he is. And man as he is, remember, was made this way by sin.

Think, too, what it has cost to make atonement for sin, and to provide a pardon and forgiveness for sinners. God's own Son had to come into the world, and take upon Himself our nature, in order to pay the price of our redemption, and deliver us from the curse of a broken law. He who was in the beginning with the Father, and by whom all things were made, had to suffer for sin—the just for the unjust—and die the death of a criminal in order to open the way to heaven for any soul. See the Lord Jesus Christ despised and rejected by men, scourged, mocked, and insulted. Behold Him bleeding on the cross of Calvary, and hear Him crying in agony, "My God, My God, why have you forsaken me?" Note how the sun was darkened, and the rocks shook at the sight, and then consider, young men, what must be the evil and guilt of sin.

Think, also, what sin has done already upon the earth. Think how it cast Adam and Eve out of Eden, brought the flood upon the old world, caused fire to come down on Sodom and Gomorrah, drowned Pharaoh and his armies in the Red Sea, destroyed the seven wicked nations of Canaan, and scattered the twelve tribes of Israel over the face of the globe. Sin alone did all this.

Think, moreover, of all the misery and sorrow that sin has caused, and is causing to this very day. Pain, disease, and death, arguments, quarrels, divisions, envy, jealousy, malice, deceit, fraud, cheating, violence, oppression, robbery, selfishness, unkindness, and ingratitude—all these are the fruits of sin. Sin is the parent of them all. It is sin that has so marred and spoiled the face of God's creation.

Young men, consider these things, and you will not wonder that we preach as we do. Surely, if you did think of them, you would break with sin forever.

Will you play with poison? Will you sport with hell? Will you take fire in your hand? Will you harbor your deadliest enemy in your arms? Will you go on living as if it mattered nothing whether your own sins were forgiven or not, whether sin ruled over you, or you over sin? Oh, awake to a sense of sin's sinfulness and danger! Remember the words of Solomon: "Fools mock at making amends for sin" (Prov. 14:9).

Hear, then, the request that I make of you this day: Pray that God would teach you the real evil of sin. If you would have your soul saved, then get up and pray.

(2) For another thing, seek to become acquainted with our Lord Jesus Christ.

This is, indeed, the principal thing in Christianity. This is the cornerstone of Christianity. Until you know this, my warnings and advice will be useless, and your endeavors— whatever they may be— will be in vain. A watch that doesn't keep track of time is as useless as religion without Christ.

But don't let me be misunderstood. It is not the mere knowing of Christ's name that I mean; it is knowing His mercy, grace, and power, the knowing Him not by the hearing of the ear, but by the experience of your hearts. I want you to know Him by faith. I want you, as Paul says, to know "the power of His resurrection; becoming like Him in His death" (Phil. 3:10). I want you to be able to say of Him, "He is my peace and my strength, my life and my consolation, my Physician and my Shepherd, my Savior and my God."

A watch that doesn't keep track of time is as useless as religion without Christ.

Why do I make such a point of this? I do it because in Christ alone "all [God's] fullness dwells" (Col. 1:19), because in Him alone there is full supply of all that we require for the necessities of our souls. By ourselves we are all poor, empty creatures—empty of righteousness and peace, empty of strength and comfort, empty of courage and patience, empty of power to stand, or go on, or make progress in this evil world. It is in Christ alone that all these things are to be found: grace, peace, wisdom, righteousness, sanctification, and redemption. It is just in proportion as we live in reliance upon Him, that we are strong Christians. It is only when self is nothing and Christ is all our confidence, that we shall do great exploits. Then only are we armed for the battle of life, and shall overcome. Then only are we prepared for the journey of life, and shall move forward. To live on Christ, to draw all from Christ, to do all in the strength of Christ, to be ever looking unto Christ; this is the true secret of spiritual prosperity. "I can do all this," says Paul, "through Christ who gives me strength" (Phil. 4:13).

Young men, I set before you Jesus Christ this day, as the treasury of your souls; and I invite you to begin by going to Him. Let this be your first step: Go to Christ. Do you want to consult friends? He is the best friend: "A friend that sticks closer than a brother" (Prov. 18:24). Do you feel unworthy because of your sins? Do not be afraid, for his blood cleanses from all sin. He says, "Though your sins are like scarlet, they shall be as white as snow: though they are as red as crimson, they shall be like wool" (Isa. 1:18). Do you feel weak and unable to follow Him? Do not be afraid, for He will give you power to become sons of God. He will give you the Holy Spirit to dwell in you, and seal you for His own. He will give you a new heart, and He will put a new spirit within you. Are you troubled or with a tendency toward certain evils? Don't be afraid, for there is no evil spirit that Jesus cannot cast out, and there is no disease of the soul that He cannot heal. Do you feel doubts and fears? Cast them aside: "Come to Me," He says; "whoever comes to me I will never drive away." He knows well the heart of a young man. He knows your trials and your temptations, your difficulties and your foes. In the days of His flesh He was like you—a young man at Nazareth. He knows by experience a young man's mind. He understands how you feel when tempted, for He also suffered when he was tempted. Surely you will have no excuse if you turn away from such a Savior and Friend as this.

Hear the request I make of you this day: If you love life, seek to become acquainted with Jesus Christ.

(3) For another thing, never forget that nothing is as important as your soul.

Your soul is eternal. It will live forever. The world and all that it contains will pass away. Firm, solid, beautiful, and well ordered as it is, the world will come to an end. "The earth and everything in it will be burned up" (2 Pet. 3:10). The works of statesmen, writers, painters, and architects are all short lived; your soul will outlive them all. The angel's voice will proclaim one day that time shall be no longer (Rev. 10:6). But that will never be said of your souls.

Try, I beg you, to realize the fact that your soul is the one thing worth living for. It is the part of you that ought always to be first considered. No place, no employment is good for you, which injures your soul. No friend, no companion deserves your confidence, who makes light of your soul's concerns. The man who hurts your person, your property, your character, only does you temporary harm. Your true enemy is the one who plots to damage your soul.

Think for a moment what you were born into this world for. Not merely to eat and drink, and indulge the desires of the flesh, not merely to dress up your body, and follow its lusts wherever they may lead you, not merely to work, and sleep, and laugh, and talk, and enjoy yourselves, and think of nothing but time. No! You were meant for something higher and better than this. You were placed here to train for eternity. Your body was only intended to be a house for your immortal spirit. It is flying in the face of God's purposes to do as many do, to make the soul a servant to the body, and not the body a servant to the soul.

Young men, God doesn't show favoritism or respect the honors bestowed by men. He rewards no man's heritage, or wealth, or rank, or position. He doesn't see with man's eyes. The poorest saint that ever died in a ghetto is nobler in His sight than the richest sinner that ever died in a palace. God does not look at riches, titles, learning, beauty, or anything of the kind. There is only one thing God does look at, and that is the immortal soul. God measures all men by one standard, one measure, one test, one criterion, and that is the state of their souls.

Do not forget this. Keep in view, morning, noon, and night the interests of your soul. Rise up each day desiring that it may prosper. Lie down each evening inquiring of yourself whether your soul has really grown. Remember Zeuxis, the great painter of old. When men asked him why he labored so intensely, and took such extreme pains with every picture, his simple answer was, "I paint for eternity." Do not be ashamed to be like him. Set your immortal soul before your mind's eye, and when men ask you why you live as you do, answer them in his spirit, "I live for my soul." Believe me, the day is coming soon when the soul will be the one thing men will think of, and the only question of importance will be this, "Is my soul lost or saved?"

(4) For another thing, remember it is possible to be a young man and yet to serve God.

I fear the snares that Satan lays for you on this point. I fear that he will succeed in filling your minds with the false notion that to be a true Christian as a youth is impossible. I have seen many carried away by this delusion. I have heard it said, "You are requiring the impossible in expecting so much Christianity from young people. Youth is no time for seriousness. Our desires are strong, and it was never intended that we should suppress them, as you wish us to do. God meant us to enjoy ourselves. There will be time enough for following Christ later." And this kind of talk is only too much encouraged by the world. The world is only too ready to wink at youthful sins. The world appears to think it a matter of course that young men must "sow their wild oats." The world seems to take it for granted young people must be irreligious, and that it is not possible for them to follow Christ.

Young men, I will ask you this simple question: Where will you find anything of such attitudes in the Word of God? Where is the chapter or verse in the Bible that will support this way of talking and reasoning of the world? Doesn't the Bible speak to old and young alike—without distinction? Is not sin still sin, whether committed at the age of twenty or at the age of fifty? Will it form the slightest excuse, in the day of judgment, to say, "I know I sinned, but I was young"? Show some common sense, I beg of you, by giving up such empty excuses. You are responsible and accountable to God from the very moment that you know right and wrong.

I know well there are many difficulties in a young man's way. However, there are always difficulties in the way of doing right. The path to heaven is always narrow, whether we are young or old.

There are difficulties, but God will give you grace to overcome them. God is not a cruel master. He will not, like Pharaoh, require you to make bricks without straw. He will make sure that the path he requires us to walk is not an impossible road. He never gives commands to man which He will not also give man the power to perform.

There are difficulties, but many a young man has overcome them in the past, and so can you. Moses was a young man with passions like yours, but see what is said of him in Scripture: "By faith Moses, when he was grown, refused to be called the son of Pharaoh's daughter; choosing rather to be mistreated with the people of God than to enjoy the pleasures of sin for a short time. He regarded disgrace for the sake of Christ as greater value than the treasures of Egypt, because he was looking ahead to his reward" (Heb. 11:24-26). Daniel was a young man when he began to serve God in Babylon. He was surrounded by temptations of every kind. He had few who stood with him, and many against him. Yet Daniel's life was so blameless and consistent, that even his enemies could find no fault in him, except "concerning the law of his God" (Dan. 6:5). And these are not solitary cases. There is a cloud of witnesses whom I could name. Time would fail me, if I were to tell you of young Isaac, young Joseph, young Joshua, young Samuel, young David, young Solomon, young Abijah, young Obadiah, young Josiah, and young Timothy. These were not angels, but men, with hearts naturally like your own. They too had obstacles to contend with, lusts to crush, trials to endure, hard roles to fill, like any of you. But young as they were, they all found it possible to serve God. Will they not all rise in judgment and condemn you, if you persist in saying it cannot be done?

Young men, try to serve God. Resist the devil when he whispers it is impossible. Try, and the Lord God of the promises will give you strength in the trying. He loves to meet those who struggle to come to Him, and He will meet you and give you the power that you feel you need. Be like the man whom Bunyan's Pilgrim saw in the Interpreter's house, go forward boldly, saying, "Write down my name." Those words of our Lord are true, though I often hear them repeated by heartless and unfeeling tongues: "Seek, and you will find; knock, and it will be opened to you" (Matt. 7:7). Difficulties that seemed like mountains shall melt away like snow in spring. Obstacles that seemed like giants in the mist of distance shall dwindle into nothing when you actually face them. The lion that blocks your path will prove to be chained and unable to harm you. If men believed God's promises more, they would never be afraid of what is required of them. But remember that little word I press upon you, and when Satan says, "You cannot be a Christian while you are young," answer him, "Get behind me, Satan. By God's help, I will try."

(5) For another thing, determine as long as you live to make the Bible your guide and adviser.

The Bible is God's merciful provision for sinful man's soul, the map by which he must steer his course if he wants to attain eternal life. All that we need to know in order to make us peaceful, holy, or happy, is richly contained there. If a young man wants to know how to begin his life well, let him hear what David says: "How can a young man keep his way pure? By living according to your word" (Ps. 119:9).

Young men, I charge you to make a habit of reading the Bible, and not to let the habit be broken. Don't let the laughter of friends, or the bad habits of the family you may live in, prevent your doing it. Determine that you will not only have a Bible, but also make time to read it too. Don't allow anyone to persuade you that it is only a book for Sunday school children and old women. It is the book from which King David got wisdom and understanding. It is the book that young Timothy knew from his childhood. Never be ashamed of reading it. Do not "despise the Word" (Prov. 13:13).

Read it with prayer for the Spirit's grace to make you understand it. It has been said, "A man may just as soon read the Scripture without eyes, as understand the spirit of it without grace."

Read it reverently, as the Word of God, not of man— believing implicitly that what it approves is right, and what it condemns is wrong. Be very sure that every doctrine that will not stand the test of Scripture is false. This will keep you from being tossed to and fro, and carried about by the dangerous opinions of these latter days. Be very sure that every practice in your life that is contrary to Scripture is sinful and must be given up. This will settle many a question of conscience, and cut the knot of many a doubt. Remember how differently two kings of Judah read the Word of God: Jehoiakim read it, and at once tore the page to pieces, and burned it in the fire (Jer. 36:23). And why? Because his heart rebelled against it, and he was resolved not to obey. Josiah read it, and at once tore his clothes, and cried mightily to the Lord (2 Chron. 34:19). And why? Because his heart was tender and obedient. He was ready to do anything that Scripture showed him was his duty. Oh that you may follow the last of these two, and not the first!

And read it regularly. This is the only way to become "mighty in the Scriptures." A quick glance at the Bible now and then does little good. At that rate you will never become familiar with its treasures, or feel the sword of the Spirit fitted to your hand in the hour of conflict. But fill your mind with Scripture by diligent reading, and you will soon discover its value and power. Verses will rise up in your hearts in the moment of temptation. Commands will suggest themselves in seasons of doubt. Promises will come across your thoughts in the time of discouragement. And thus you will experience the truth of David's words, "I have hidden your word in my heart, that I might not sin against you "(Ps. 119:11); and of Solomon's words, "When you walk, they will guide you; when you sleep, they will watch over you; and when you awake, they will speak to you" (Prov. 6:22).

I dwell on these things more because this is an age of reading. There seems to be no end of making books, though few of them are really profitable. There seems a rage for cheap printing and publishing. Newspapers of every sort abound, and the tone of some, which have the widest circulation, speaks badly for the taste of the age. Amid the flood of dangerous reading, I plead for my Master's book. I call upon you not to forget the book of the soul. Don't let newspapers, novels, and romances be read, while the prophets and Apostles lie despised by comparison. Do not let the exciting and sensual swallow up your attention, while the edifying and the sanctifying can find no place in your mind.

Young men, give the Bible the honor due to it every day you live. Whatever you read, read that first. And beware of bad books: there are plenty in this day. Take heed what you read. I suspect there is more harm done to souls in this way than most people have an idea is possible. Value all books in proportion to the extent they agree with Scripture. Those that are nearest to it are the best, and those that are farthest from it—and most contrary to it—the worst.

(6) For another thing, never make an intimate friend of any one who is not a friend of God.

Understand that I am not speaking of acquaintances. I don't mean that you ought to have nothing to do with any but true Christians. To take such a line is neither possible nor desirable in this world. Christianity requires no man to be rude.

Never be satisfied with the friendship of any one who will not be useful to your soul.

But I do advise you to be very careful in your choice of friends. Don't open all your heart to a man merely because he is clever, agreeable, good-natured, fun, and kind. These things are all very well in their way, but they are not everything. Never be satisfied with the friendship of any one who will not be useful to your soul.

Believe me, the importance of this advice cannot be overrated. There is no telling the harm that is done by associating with godless companions and friends. The devil has few better helps in ruining a man's soul. Grant him this help, and he cares little for all the armor with which you may be armed against him. Good education, early habits of morality, sermons, books, and words of parents will be of little benefit to you, if you cling to ungodly friends. You may resist many open temptations and refuse many obvious snares; but once you take up a bad companion, the devil is content. That awful chapter which describes Amnon's wicked conduct towards Tamar, almost begins with these words, "But Amnon had a friend, a very shrewd man" (2 Sam. 13:3).

You must remember, we are all creatures of imitation: precept may teach us, but it is example that draws us. There is something in all of us that makes us disposed to catch the ways of those with whom we live; and the more we like them, the stronger that inclination grows. Without our being aware of it, they influence our tastes and opinions, we gradually give up what they dislike and take up what they like in order to become closer friends with them. And, worst of all, we catch their ways in things that are wrong far quicker than in things that are right. Health, unhappily, is not contagious, but disease is. It is far easier to catch a chill than to impart warmth; and to make each other's religion dwindle away, than grow and prosper.

Young men, I ask you to take these things to heart. Before you let any one become your constant companion, before you get into the habit of telling him everything, and going to him in all your troubles and all your pleasures, before you do this, just think of what I have been saying; ask yourself, "Will this be a useful friendship to me or not?"

"Bad company" does indeed "corrupt good character" (1 Cor. 15:33). I wish that text were written in hearts of all young men. Good friends are among our greatest blessings. They may keep us back from much evil, help us along our way, speak an encouraging word when needed, draw us upward, and spur us on. But a bad friend is a positive misfortune, a weight continually dragging us down, and chaining us to earth. Keep close company with an unsaved man, and it is more than probable you will in the end become like him. That is the general result of all such friendships. The good go down to the bad, and the bad do not come up to the good. The world's proverb is only too correct: "Clothes and company tell true tales about character." And "Show me who a man lives with," says the Spaniards, "and I will show you what he is."

I dwell upon this point, because it has more to do with your prospects in life than first appears. If you ever marry, it is more than probable you will choose a wife from among your circle of friends. If Jehoshaphat's son Jehoram had not formed a friendship with Ahab's family, he would most likely not have married Ahab's daughter. And who can estimate the importance of a right choice in marriage? It is a step that, according to the old saying, "either makes a man or ruins him." Your happiness in both lives may depend on it. Your wife will either help your soul or harm it; there is no medium. She will either fan the flame of Christianity in your heart, or throw cold water upon it and make it burn low. She will either be wings or handcuffs, a rein or a spur to your Christianity, according to her character. Whoever finds a good wife does indeed "find a good thing;" so if you have the least desire to find one, be very careful how you choose your friends.

Do you ask me what kind of friends you shall choose? Choose friends who will benefit your soul, friends whom you can really respect, friends whom you would like to have near you on your death-bed, friends who love the Bible and are not afraid to speak to you about it, friends such as you will not be ashamed of owning at the coming of Christ and the day of judgment. Follow the example that David sets for you when he says, "I am a friend to all who fear God, to all who follow His precepts" (Ps. 119:63). Remember the words of Solomon: "He who walks with the wise grows wise; but a companion of fools suffers harm" (Prov. 13:20). But depend on it, bad company in this life is the sure way to procure worse company in the life to come.

Choose friends who will benefit
your soul, friends whom you can
really respect, friends whom you
would like to have near you on your
death-bed, friends who love the
Bible and are not afraid to speak
to you about it.

Study Guide on
Chapter 3

1. Ryle gives six general words of counsel, or advice to young men. List them.

2. The first word of advice Ryle gives is to "try to get a clear view of the evil of sin." All of us have done something that we may have thought, "It's not a big deal" (Examples: a statement that is "mostly true", the joke you shouldn't have laughed at, the attitude you gave your parents). Ryle warns to not "let the devil succeed in persuading you that sin is a small matter." Give at least three reasons why Ryle says that sin always a big deal.

3. Whatever the circumstances, Ryle urges you to begin by turning to Jesus. He reminds you that Jesus knows your heart—all your trials and temptations, difficulties and foes—because he was a young man too. Have you ever thought about the fact that Jesus knows by experience the things that go on in your mind?

4. Why is that a game changer? Why should that truth make a difference?

5. How is your soul different from your body? Why does the author say it is more important?

6. How do the examples of Moses and Daniel—along with Isaac, Joshua, Samuel, David, Timothy, and others—prove that you can do great things for God while still a young man?

7. How are *you* serving God as a young man?

8. Ryle gives several words of advice in relation to making the Bible your guide and advisor. Name at least four things he says you should do in regards to God's Word.

9. At the end of chapter 3 – section 5, Ryle says, "Do not let newspapers, novels, and romances be read, while the prophets and Apostles lie despised by comparison. . . . Young men, give the Bible the honor due to it every day you live. Whatever you read, read that first." What would need to change in your life in order for this to be a reality? Do you need to spend less time on the computer? Cut down your gaming? Get up earlier? Skip one TV show a day?

10. Ryle urges you to never make an intimate friend of anyone who is not a friend of God, and he says that the " importance of this advice cannot be overrated." Based on the rest of that section, give at least three reasons why this principle is so important.

11. At the end of chapter 3, Ryle gives qualities of what kind of friend you should choose. List three:

12. Do you have friends that fit that description?

13. If you do, what can you do to deepen and strengthen those friendships? If you don't, what can you do to change that and to find such quality friends?

Chapter 4:
Special Rules for Young Men

IN THE LAST place, I will set down some particular rules of conduct that I strongly advise all young men to follow.

(1) For one thing, resolve at once, by God's help, to break off every known sin, however small.

Look within, each one of you. Examine your own hearts. Do you see there any habit or custom which you know to be wrong in the sight of God? If you do, don't delay a moment in attacking it. Resolve at once to lay it aside. Nothing darkens the eyes of the mind so much, and deadens the conscience so surely, as an allowed sin. It may be a little one, but it is not the less dangerous because it is small. A small leak will sink a great ship, and a small spark will kindle a great fire, and a little allowed sin in like manner will ruin an immortal soul. Take my advice, and never spare a little sin. Israel was commanded to slay every Canaanite, both great and small. Act on the same principle, and show no mercy to little sins. Well says the book of Song of Songs, "Take us the foxes, the little foxes, that spoil the vines" (Song of Songs 2:15).

You can be sure that no wicked man ever meant to be so wicked at his first beginnings. But he began with allowing himself some little transgression, and that led on to something greater, and that in time produced something greater still, and thus he became the miserable being that he now is. When Hazael heard from Elisha of the horrible acts that he would one day do, he said with astonishment, "How could your servant, a mere dog, accomplish such a feat?" (2 Kings 8:13). But he allowed sin to take root in his heart, and in the end he did them all.

Young men, resist sin in its beginnings. They may look small and insignificant, but mind what I say. Resist them. Make no compromise. Let no sin lodge quietly and undisturbed in your heart. There is nothing finer than the point of a needle, but when it has made a hole, it draws all the thread after it. Remember the Apostle's words, "A little yeast works through the whole batch of dough" (1 Cor. 5:6).

Many a young man could tell you with sorrow and shame, that he can traces the path of ruin of all his worldly prospects to the point I speak of—to giving way to sin in its beginnings. He began habits of falsehood and dishonesty in little things, and they grew upon him. Step by step, he has gone on from bad to worse, till he has done things that at one time he would have thought impossible; till at last he has lost his place, lost his character, lost his comfort, and nearly lost his soul. He allowed a gap in the wall of his conscience, because it seemed a little one, and once allowed, that gap grew larger every day—until eventually the whole wall seemed to come down.

Look within, each one of you.
Examine your own hearts. Do you
see there any habit or custom which
you know to be wrong in the sight
of God?

Remember this especially in matters of truth and honesty. Be careful of even the least syllable spoken. "Whoever can be trusted with very little can be trusted with much, and whoever is dishonest with very little will also be dishonest with much" (Luke 16:10). Whatever the world may like to say, there are no little sins. All great buildings are made up of little parts, and the first stone is as important as any other. All habits are formed by a series of little acts, and the first little act is of mighty consequence. The axe in the fable only begged the trees to let him have one little piece of wood to make a handle, and he would never trouble them any more. He got it, and then he soon cut them all down. The devil only wants to get the wedge of a little allowed sin into your heart, and you will soon be all his own. It is a wise saying of old William Bridge, "There is nothing small between us and God, for God is an infinite God."

There are two ways of coming down from the top of a church steeple; one way is to jump down, and the other is to walk down by the steps—but both will lead you to the bottom. So also there are two ways of going to hell; one way is to walk into it with your eyes open, and few people do that; the other is to go down by the steps of little sins, and that way, I fear, is only too common. Put up with a few little sins, and you will soon want a few more. Even a heathen could say, "Who was ever content with only one sin?" If you put up with little sins in your life, then your path will grow worse and worse every year. Well did Jeremy Taylor describe the progress of sin in a man:

"First it startles him, then it becomes pleasing, then easy, then delightful, then frequent, then habitual, then a way of life! Then the man feels no guilt, then is obstinate, then resolves never to repent, and then he is condemned."

Young men, if you would not come to this, remember the rule I give you this day: Resolve at once to break off every known sin.

(2) For another thing, resolve, by God's help, to shun everything that may prove an occasion of sin.

It is an excellent saying, "Whoever would be safe from the acts of evil, must widely avoid the occasions." It is not enough that we determine to commit no sin; we must carefully keep at a distance from all that leads us into it. By this test we ought to examine our ways of spending our time, the books that we read, the friends that we spend time with, the places that we go. We must not content ourselves with saying, "There is nothing wrong here." We must go further, and say, "Is there anything here which may cause me to sin?"

Remember, this is one great reason why idleness is to be avoided. It is not that doing nothing is of itself so positively wicked; it is the opportunity it provides for evil thoughts and empty fantasies; it is the wide door it opens for Satan to throw in the seeds of bad things; it is this which is mainly to be feared. If David had not given occasion to the devil, by lounging on his housetop at Jerusalem instead of at the battlefield with his armies, he may never have committed adultery with Bathsheba or murdered Uriah.

This, too, is one great reason why worldly amusements are so objectionable. It may be difficult, in some instances, to show that they are, in themselves, positively unscriptural and wrong. But there is little difficulty in showing that the tendency of almost all of them is most injurious to the soul. They sow the seeds of an earthly and sensual frame of mind. They war against the life of faith. They promote an unhealthy and unnatural craving after excitement. They minister to the lust of the flesh, and the lust of the eye, and the pride of life (1 John 2:16). They dim the view of heaven and eternity, and give a false colour to the things of time. They lead the heart away from a desire for private prayer, and Scripture-reading, and calm communion with God. The man who mingles in them gives Satan the advantage. He has a battle to fight, and he gives his enemy the help of sun, and wind, and hill. It would be strange indeed if he did not find himself continually defeated.

Young men, endeavour, as much as you can, to steer clear of everything that might injure your soul. People may say you are too conscientious, too particular, and ask you where is the great harm of such and such things? But don't listen to them. It is dangerous to play tricks with sharp tools; it is far more dangerous to take liberties with your immortal soul. He that would be safe must not come near the brink of danger. He must look on his heart as a barrel of gunpowder, and be cautious not to handle one spark of temptation more than he can help.

What is the point of your praying, "Lead us not into temptation," unless you are yourselves careful not to run into it? What is the point of praying, "Deliver us from evil," unless you show a desire to keep out of evil's way? Look at the example of Joseph. Not only did he refuse the invitation to sin from his master's wife, but also he showed his good sense in refusing to be "with her" at all (Gen. 39:10). Take to heart the advice of Solomon: Be sure to "not set foot on the path of wickedness," but also be sure to "avoid it, do not travel on it, turn from it and go your own way" (Prov. 4:14, 15). Don't just avoid drunkenness, but be sure not to be enticed by the power of wine (Prov. 23:31). The man who took the vow of a Nazarite in Israel, not only vowed to take no wine, but he even abstained from grapes in any shape whatever. "*Hate what is evil*," says Paul to the Romans (Rom. 12:9)— not merely "*do not do* what is evil." "Flee the evil desires of youth," he writes to Timothy—get away from them as far as possible (2 Tim. 2:22). How important are such warnings! Dinah just had to go out among the wicked Shechemites, to see their ways, and she lost her virginity. Lot just had to pitch his tent near sinful Sodom, and he lost everything but his life.

Young men, be wise! Don't always be trying to see how near you can allow the enemy of souls to come, and yet still escape him. Instead, hold him at arm's length.

Try to keep clear of temptation as far as possible, and this will be a great help to keeping clear of sin.

(3) For another thing, resolve never to forget the eye of God.

The eye of God! Think of that. Everywhere—in every house, in every field, in every room, in every company, alone or in a crowd—the eye of God is always upon you. "The eyes of the LORD are everywhere, keeping watch on the wicked and the good" (Prov. 15:3), and they are eyes that read hearts as well as actions.

Make every effort, I beg you all, to realize this fact. Remember that you have to deal with an all-seeing God—a God who never slumbers nor sleeps, a God who understands all your thoughts, and with whom the night shines as the day. You may leave your father's home and go away, like the prodigal, into a far country, and think that there is nobody to watch your conduct; but the eye and ear of God are there before you. You may deceive your parents or employers—you may tell them falsehoods, and be one thing before their faces and another behind their backs—but you cannot deceive God. He knows you through and through. He heard what you said as you came here today. He knows what you are thinking of at this minute. He has set your most secret sins in the light of His countenance, and they will one day come out before the world to your shame, unless you watch out.

How little is this really felt! How many things are

done continually, which men would never do if they thought they were seen! How many matters are transacted in the rooms of imagination, which would never be allowed to occur in the light of day! Yes, men entertain thoughts in private, and say words in private, and do acts in private, which they would be ashamed and blush to have exposed before the world. The sound of a footstep coming has stopped many a deed of wickedness. A knock at the door has caused many an evil work to be quickly suspended, and hurriedly laid aside. But oh, what miserable folly is all this! There is an all-seeing Witness with us wherever we go. Lock the door, draw down the blind, shut the shutters, turn out the light; it matters not, it makes no difference; God is everywhere. You cannot shut Him out, or prevent His seeing. "Nothing in all creation is hidden from God's sight" (Heb. 4:13). Well did young Joseph understand this when his master's wife tempted him. There was no one in the house to see them, no human eye to witness against him, but Joseph was one who lived as seeing Him that is invisible: "How could I do such a wicked thing," said he, "and sin against God?" (Gen. 39:9).

Young men, I ask you all to read Psalm 139. I advise you all to learn it by heart. Make it the test of all your dealings in this world's business. Say to yourself often, "Do I remember that God sees me?"

Live as in the sight of God. This is what Abraham did—he walked before Him. This is what Enoch did—he walked with Him. This is what heaven itself will be—the eternal presence of God. Do nothing you would not like God to see. Say nothing you would not like God to hear. Write nothing you would not like God to read. Go no place you would not like God to find you. Read no book of which you would not like God to say, "Show it to Me." Never spend your time in such a way that you would not like to have God say, "What are you doing?"

(4) For another thing, be diligent in the practice of your Christianity.

Be regular in going to church—whenever it is open for prayer and preaching, and it is in your power to attend. Be regular in keeping the Lord's day holy, and determine that God's day out of the seven shall always be given to its rightful owner.

I would not leave any false impression on your minds. Do not go away and say I told you that going to church made up the whole of Christianity. I tell you no such thing. I have no wish to see you grow up as legalists and Pharisees. If you think that merely carrying your body to a certain house, at certain times, on a certain day in the week, will make you a Christian and prepare you to meet God, I tell you flatly that you are miserably deceived. All services without heart-service are unprofitable and pointless. The only true worshipers of God are those who "worship the Father in the Spirit and in truth . . . they are the kind of worshipers the Father seeks" (John 4:23).

Your soul's eternal well-being most certainly does not depend on the performace of Christian rituals, but it is certain that without them, as a general rule, your soul will not do well.

But the practices of Christianity are not to be despised because they are not saviours. Gold is not food—you cannot eat it—but you would not therefore say it is useless and throw it away. Your soul's eternal well-being most certainly does not depend on the performace of Christian rituals, but it is certain that without them, as a general rule, your soul will not do well. God might take all who are saved to heaven in a chariot of fire, as He did Elijah, but He does not do so. He might teach them all by visions, and dreams, and miraculous interventions, without requiring them to read or think for themselves, but He does not do so. And why not? Because He is a God that works by means and mechanisms, and it is His law and will that in all man's dealings with him certain instruments shall be used. Only a fool would think of building a house without ladders and scaffolding, and in the same way, no wise man will despise the habits of a Christian.

I dwell on this point because Satan will try hard to fill your minds with arguments against the traits and habits of a Christian. He will draw your attention to the people who use them and are no better for the using. "See there," he will whisper," observe how those who go to church are no better than those who stay away?" But do not let this move you. It is never fair to argue against a thing because it is improperly used. It does not follow that the practices of Christianity can do no good because many do them but get no good from them. Medicine is not to be despised because many take it and do not recover their health. No man would think of giving up eating and drinking because others choose to eat and drink improperly, and so make themselves sick. The value of the Christian habits, like other things, depends, in a great measure, on the manner and spirit in which we use them.

I dwell on this point too because of the strong anxiety I feel that every young man should regularly hear the preaching of Christ's gospel. I cannot emphasize enough how important I think this is. By God's blessing, the ministry of the gospel might be the means of converting your soul, of leading you to a saving knowledge of Christ, of making you a child of God in deed and in truth. This would be cause for eternal thankfulness indeed. This would be an event over which angels would rejoice. But even if this were not the case, there is a restraining power and influence in the ministry of the gospel, under which I earnestly desire every young man to be brought. There are thousands whom it keeps back from evil, though it has not yet turned them to God. It has made them far better members of society, though it has not yet made them true Christians. There is a certain kind of mysterious power in the faithful preaching of the gospel, which has an effect even on those who listen to it without receiving it into their hearts. To hear sin revealed for what it is, and holiness lifted up, to hear Christ exalted, and the works of the devil denounced, to hear the kingdom of heaven and its blessedness described, and the world and its emptiness exposed; to hear this week after week, Sunday after Sunday, is seldom without good effect to the soul. It makes it far harder afterwards to run out and commit blatant sin. It acts as a wholesome check upon a man's heart. This, I believe, is one way in which that promise of God is made good, "My word...will not return to Me empty" (Isa. 55:11). There is much truth in that strong saying of Whitefield, "The gospel keeps many a man from going to jail and from being hanged, if it does not keep him from hell."

Let me here name another point that is closely connected with this subject. Let nothing ever tempt you to become a Christian who does not make every effort to attend church and devote the Sabbath to the Lord. I press this on your attention. Make up your mind to give all your Sundays to the Lord. A spirit of disregard for this day is growing up among us with fearful rapidity, and not least among young men. Sunday vacations, Sunday visiting, Sunday excursions—to the exclusion of church attendance and honoring the Lord—are becoming every year more common than they were, and are doing infinite harm to souls.

Young men, be jealous on this point. Whether you live in town or country, take up a decided line: resolve not to miss church and the fellowship of God's people. Don't let the plausible argument of "needing to sleep in to rest your body," the bad example of those around you, the invitation of friends—don't let any of these things—move you to depart from this firm rule: that Sundays are for honoring God and fellowshipping in church with His people.

Once you stop viewing Sundays as special and important in your life, you will eventually stop caring for your soul. The steps that lead to this conclusion are easy and common. Begin with not honoring the Lord's day, and you will soon not honor God's people. Cease to honor God's people, and you will soon cease to honor God's book. Cease to honor God's book, and by and by you will give God no honor at all. Let a man lay the foundation of having no respect for the worship of God or the fellowship of His people, and I am never surprised if he finishes with no God. It is a remarkable saying of Judge Hale, "Of all the persons who were convicted of capital crimes while he was judge, he found only a few who would not confess, when questioned, that they began their career of wickedness by a neglect of the church and God's people."

Young men, you may have friends who forget to honor the Lord's day; but resolve, by God's help, that you will always remember to keep it special. Honor it by a regular attendance at some place where the gospel is preached. Settle down under a faithful ministry, and once settled, let your place in church never be empty. Believe me, you will find a special blessing following you if you "call the Sabbath a delight and the Lord's holy day honorable, and if you honor it by not going your own way and not doing as you please or speaking idle words, then you will find your joy in the Lord " (Isa. 58:13,14). And one thing is very certain: your feelings about the Lord's day will always be a test and criterion of your fitness for heaven. Worship and fellowship on the Sabbath are a foretaste and fragment of heaven. The man who finds them a burden and not a privilege, may be sure that his heart stands in need of a mighty change.

(5) For another thing, resolve that wherever you are, you will pray.

Prayer is the life-breath of a man's soul. Without it, we may have a name and be counted as Christians, but we are dead in the sight of God. The feeling that we must cry to God for mercy and peace is a mark of grace, and the habit of spreading before Him our soul's needs is evidence that we have been adopted by God. And prayer is the appointed way to obtain the relief of our spiritual necessities. It opens the treasury, and sets the fountain flowing. If we do not have, it is because we do not ask (James 4:2).

And here it is, I say it with sorrow, here it is that men fall short so miserably. Few indeed are to be found who pray. Many go down on their knees, and say a form of prayer perhaps, but few genuinely pray—few cry out God, few call upon the Lord, few seek as if they wanted to find, few knock as if they hungered and thirsted, few wrestle, few strive with God earnestly for an answer, few give Him no rest, few continue in prayer, few persevere in prayer, few pray always without ceasing, and don't give up. Yes: few pray! It is just one of the things assumed as a matter of course, but seldom practiced. Prayer is a thing that is everybody's business, but in fact hardly anybody actually performs.

Young men, believe me, if your soul is to be saved, you must pray. God has no speechless children. If you are to resist the world, the flesh, and the devil, you must pray. It is pointless to look for strength in the hour of trial, if it has not been asked for. You may be thrown in with those who never do it, you may have to sleep in the same room with some one who never asks anything of God, but still, mark my words, you must pray.

I can certainly believe you find it difficulties to do— difficult to find opportunities, and times, and places to pray. I dare not lay down strict rules on such points as these. I leave them to your own conscience. You must be guided by circumstances. Our Lord Jesus Christ prayed on a mountain; Isaac prayed in the fields; Hezekiah turned his face to the wall as he lay upon his bed; Daniel prayed by the riverside; Peter, the Apostle, on the house-top. I have heard of young men praying in stables and haylofts. All that I contend for is this: You must know what it is to enter into your closet (Matt. 6:6). There must be stated times when you speak to God face-to-face. You must every day have your times for prayer. You must pray.

Without this, all advice and counsel is useless. This is the piece of spiritual armor that Paul names last in his list of armor in Ephesians 6, but it is in truth first in value and importance. This is the meat that you must daily eat, if you wish to travel safely through the wilderness of this life. It is only in the strength of this that you will make progress onward towards the mountain of God. I have heard it said that some people who grind metal sometimes wear a magnetic mouthpiece at their work, which catches all the fine dust that flies around them, prevents it entering their lungs, and so saves their lives. Prayer is the mouthpiece that you must wear continually, or else you will never work on uninjured in the unhealthy atmosphere of this sinful world. You must pray.

Young men, you can be sure no time is so well spent as that which a man spends upon his knees. Make time for this, whatever your situation may be. Think of David, king of Israel, who said, "Evening, and morning, and at noon, will I pray, and cry aloud: and He will hear my voice" (Ps. 55:17). Think of Daniel. He had all the business of a kingdom on his hands, yet he prayed three times a day. This was the secret of his safety in wicked Babylon. Think of Solomon. He begins his reign with prayer for help and assistance, and this results in his wonderful prosperity. Think of Nehemiah. He could find time to pray to the God of heaven, even when standing in the presence of his master, King Artaxerxes. Think of the example these godly men have left you, and go and do likewise.

Oh that the Lord may give you all the spirit of grace and supplication! "Have you not just called to Me: 'My father, my friend from my youth'? " (Jer. 3:4). I would gladly consent that all the rest of my message should be forgotten, if only this doctrine of the importance of prayer might be impressed on your hearts.

Study Guide on
Chapter 4

1. The author discusses five rules of conduct that he strongly advises all young men to follow. List those five rules.

2. Take a few minutes to follow the author's command to "look within...Examine your own heart. Do you see there any habit or custom which you know is wrong in the sight of God?" Is there an "allowed sin" that you need to "resolve at once to lay aside"?

3. The next rule of conduct suggests that one "shun everything which may prove an occasion of sin." What does Ryle mean by that?

4. How could this advice be helpful to someone?

5. How could this advice lead you to being legalistic like the Pharisees?

6. Ryle advises you to remember that the eye of God is always upon you. He says that many things are done which men would never do it they thought they were seen. Can you think of something you did, that you would never have done, if you really felt and understood that God was watching you

at that moment?

7. Reread the last paragraph of Ryle's third rule—where he offers a variety of practical ways to apply his exhortation to "never forget the eye of God". Which one of these stands out to you the most as something that you need to apply to your own life more?

8. What reason does Ryle give for being diligent about making the most of "the practice of your Christianity" – in this case, specifically, church involvement?

9. How will these reasons be important for you to remember when you're older and your parents aren't there to "make" you go to church?

10. In making his fifth point, Ryle offers several reasons why prayer is important. Write down at least three of them.

11. Chapter 4 – section 5 says: "Yes, few pray! It is just one of the things assumed as a matter of course, but seldom practiced. Prayer is a thing that is everybody's business, but in fact hardly anybody actually performs." To what extent would you say the message of this quote is true in your own life?

12. How can you move from being a person who says that prayer is important to being a person who proves that prayer is important by actually spending more time in prayer?

*Go then, young men, and resolve
this day to remember your Creator
in the days of your youth.*

Chapter 5:
Conclusion

A ND NOW I hurry towards a conclusion. I have said things that many perhaps will not like, and not receive, but I appeal to your consciences: *Are they not true?*

Young men, you have all consciences. Though corrupt and ruined by the fall as we are, each of us has a conscience. In a corner of each heart there sits a witness for God, a witness who condemns when we do wrong, and approves when we do right. To that witness I make my appeal this day: *Are not the things that I have been saying true?*

Go then, young men, and resolve this day to remember your Creator in the days of your youth (Ecc. 12:1). Before the day of grace is past, before your conscience has become hardened by age and deadened by repeated trampling under foot, while you have strength, and time, and opportunities, go and join yourself to the Lord in an everlasting covenant not to be forgotten. The Spirit will not always strive. The voice of conscience will become feebler and fainter every year you continue to resist it. The Athenians said to Paul, "We will hear you again on this matter," but they had heard him for the last time (Acts 17:32). Make haste, and don't delay. Linger and hesitate no more.

Think of the unspeakable comfort you will give to parents, relations, and friends, if you take my counsel. They have expended time, money, and health to raise you and make you what you are. Surely they deserve some consideration at your hands. Who can know the joy and gladness that young people have it in their power to produce? Who can tell the anxiety and sorrow that sons like Esau, and Hophni, and Phinehas, and Absalom may cause? Truly indeed does Solomon say, "A wise son brings joy to his father, but a foolish son brings grief to his mother" (Prov. 10:1). Oh, consider these things, and give God your heart! Let it not be said of you at last, as it is of many, that your "youth was a mistake, your manhood a struggle, and your old age a regret."

Think of the good you might be doing for the world. Almost all the most eminent saints of God sought the Lord early in life. Moses, Samuel, David, Daniel—all served God from their youth. God seems to delight in putting special honor upon young servants. And what might we confidently expect, if young men in our own day would dedicate the springtime of their lives to God? Workers are wanted now in almost every great and good cause, and cannot be found. Machinery of every kind for spreading truth exists, but there are not hands to work it.

Money is easier to obtain for doing good than men. Ministers are wanted for new churches, missionaries are wanted for new fields, helpers are wanted for neglected ministries, and teachers are wanted for new schools. Many a good cause is standing still merely because of a lack of volunteers. The supply of godly, faithful, trustworthy men, for positions like those I have named, is far below the demand.

Young men of the present day, you are wanted for God. This is an age of activity. We are shaking off some of our past selfishness. Men no longer sleep the sleep of apathy and indifference about others, as their forefathers did. They are beginning to be ashamed of thinking, like Cain, "Am I my brother's keeper?" A wide field of usefulness is open before you, if you are only willing to enter upon it. The harvest is great, and the laborers are few. Be zealous for good works. Come, come and be used by the Lord against the evil of this age.

This is, in some sort, to be like God—not only good, but doing good (Ps. 119:68). This is the way to follow the steps of your Lord and Savior, "Who went about doing good" (Acts 10:38). This is to live as David did; he "served his own generation" (Acts 13:36).

And who can doubt that this is the path that makes an immortal soul beautiful? Wouldn't you rather leave this world like Josiah, grieved by all, than depart like Jehoram, "to no one's regret"? (2 Chron. 21:20). Is it better to be idle and frivolous, to live for your body, your selfishness, your lusts, and your pride, or to spend and be spent in the glorious cause of usefulness to your fellow men—to be a blessing to your country and the world, to be the friend of the prisoner and the captive, to be a burning and a shining light, an epistle of Christ, known and read of all men, the inspiration of every Christian heart that comes across your path? Oh, who can doubt? Who can for one moment doubt?

Young men, consider your responsibilities. Think of the privilege and luxury of doing good. Resolve this day to be useful. Give your hearts at once to Christ.

Think, lastly, of the happiness that will come to your own soul if you serve God— happiness along the way, as you travel through life, and happiness in the end, when the journey is over. Believe me, whatever foolish notions you may have heard, there is a reward for the righteous even in this world. Godliness indeed holds promise for this life, as well as for that which is to come. There is a solid peace in feeling that God is your friend. There is a real satisfaction in knowing that however great your unworthiness, you are complete in Christ, that you have an enduring inheritance, that you have chosen that good part which shall not be taken from you.

The backslider in heart may well be filled with his own ways, but "the good man will be rewarded for his" (Prov. 14:14). The path of the worldly man grows darker and darker every year that he lives, but the path of the Christian is as a shining light, brighter and brighter to the very end. His sun is just rising when the sun of the worldly is setting forever. His best things are all beginning to blossom and bloom forever, when those of the worldly are all slipping out of his hands and passing away.

Young men, these things are true. Listen to this word of exhortation. Be persuaded. Take up the cross. Follow Christ. Yield yourselves unto God.

Study Guide on Chapter 5

1. In this chapter the author gives several reasons why you should pay attention to all that he has said. What are three of the reasons he gives?

2. At the beginning of chapter 5, Ryle says that he has said things that "many perhaps will not like, and not receive" but asks you to check your conscience and ask yourself, "Are they not true?" What things from this book did you "not like", and perhaps want to reject?

3. Bring these before God, and ask him: *Are they true?* Or not? (Though Ryle is a godly man, he's not God!) It is possible that you may rightly disagree with something he has said. However, it's important to bring those things before God in prayer, and to discern why it is that you disagree. Is it because your flesh doesn't want to agree? Or is it because Ryle's point doesn't necessarily agree with Scripture?

4. What points from this book challenged you most to grow and change as a young man? How will you be different—in your thoughts and/or actions—as a result of reading this book? (List at least three things.)

Made in the USA
San Bernardino, CA
02 September 2016